To:

_____

From:

_____

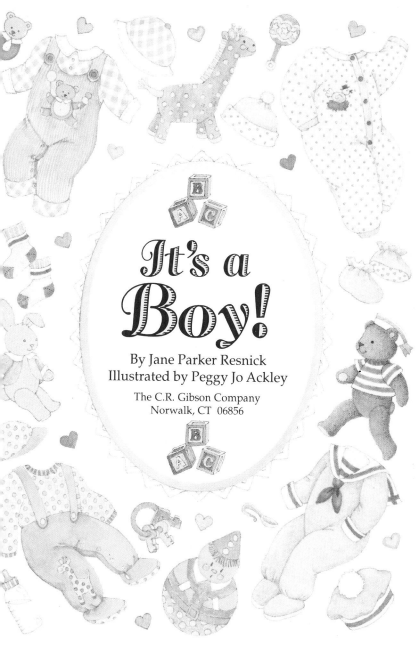

It's a Boy!

By Jane Parker Resnick
Illustrated by Peggy Jo Ackley

The C.R. Gibson Company
Norwalk, CT 06856

For the first few minutes of your baby boy's life the world must be a frightening space of alien air and foreign light. But you are there to hold him and soothe him, to make his world a place of pleasure, not pain. And so you always will be. No matter what scares him, he will never be too old for your comfort or too big for your arms.

A baby boy is asleep in his crib.
Tiptoe in to take a peek.
What do you see?
Cheeks of pink beneath a blanket of blue,
Barely a breath, hardly a sigh.
But in that bed is the beginning of life
Beautiful and perfect,
Created just for you.

Peek in the room where your baby sleeps. How sweet. How neat. For now. But it will be a growing boy's room one day, and when you enter, he'll say, "Don't touch my stuff! And don't throw away the good things!"

As if you would dream of rearranging the baseball cards or the water pistols. Or last year's lizard or his model plane that's missing a wing.

A boy needs his baseball glove nearby, and his lightning bugs kept in a jar and his bicycle horn by the side of the bed. What sacred territory, a boy's room is...with magic in the rock collection and mysteries under the bed.

  Today, your family has one more person in it. Small, yes. Sleeping, mostly. But indispensable. Yesterday, the circle of your love did not include this baby boy, and yet it was complete. Now, the circle is so lacking without him.

  Your love expanded at the moment of his birth, drew him in, surrounded him and will never let him go.

Just when you thought
Life had some order.
Just when you thought
Peace was at hand,
Here comes a baby boy.
Give him an hour,
And he'll take your morning.
Give him your days,
And he'll take your nights.
Time is just space to grow in,
When you're a newborn baby boy.

Why is it that once a boy learns to walk, he runs? He slams doors, never shuts them? Races his bike, never rides? Attacks his food, never eats? Crashes into furniture, never sits? Skids to a halt, never stops? Bursts into rooms, never enters? Drives into play, never pauses? And finally, plunges into sleep, but never rests?

Ask him and he'll tell you, "Just because!" And there never was a better answer.

This baby boy will change your hours. He'll even make holidays seem new. So picture this, Valentine's Day, from your son to you...

He made it at school from bits and pieces of doilies, ribbons and red paper. It's heart-shaped or was, until its crumpled journey home in his pocket. It smells of paste and crayon, the E is backwards and the Y is upside down. But the message is "I Love You" and there's no more beautiful work of art.

A boy is a mystery with clues hidden in the corners of his mouth and in the gleam of his eyes... the answers are all yet to come. And therein lies the fun.

Your life is going to be livelier now.
Your days a little longer and a little
noisier too. You're going to see the
world from a new point of view—
curiosity is going to get the best of you.
For with a boy, your mind will never
be still, your hours will always be busy,
your days will never be empty, and
your heart will ever be filled.

Today, little man,
We will have a piggyback ride.
Cling to me and I will raise you,
As your laughter lifts my heart;
Cling to me and I will carry you
On the shoulders of my love.

Your baby's life is in your hands now. What he sees, he views through your eyes. What he knows, he learns from you. He'll watch your behavior and mimic it. He'll study your values and absorb them. So giving him life was just the beginning. Teaching him gives your life meaning.

*A boy is a quick change artist,
a chameleon in many-colored clothing.
Angel for a minute, devil for a second;
quiet as a kitten, loud as a hyena.
Quicksilver one moment, molasses the next,
he turns tears to laughter, anger to joy.
What can you expect: He's a boy!*

While the baby sleeps,
It's the parents who dream
Of bicycles and fishing poles,
Flying kites and swimming holes.
For while the child sleeps, everyone knows
That baseball games and pollywogs,
Climbing trees and catching frogs
Cannot be far off, as a little boy grows.

It's wake-up time for your baby boy. What's new today? Well, lifting his head to meet the world. Squirming to the edge of the crib. Shrieking loud enough to wake the cat.

Sighing as sweetly as a summer breeze. What's next? Rolling over, sitting up...every day's a challenge met. A boy, will fill your days in happy surprising ways.

Funny face is what you say,
Because his face is round and pink.
But "beautiful" is what you really think.
"Annoying" you declare,
Because he cries when you're asleep.
But "precious" is the thought you keep.
"Impossible" you claim
when he's hungry all the time,
But "priceless" is the word
that really comes to mind.
"Hopeless" is what you swear
when he won't take a nap,
But "blessed" is what you believe,
caught in the baby trap.

Now, how will you put the baby
In another room?
When all these months
He's been sleeping
In your loving womb.
And how will you feed him
With a spoon?
Weaning him from breast to bottle,
To lunch at noon.
Then, how will you tell him
He's separate from you?
When he's the reason
You get up each day.
And your life is his
In every way.

The joy you feel with the birth of this son is not easy to describe. It's not mere delight. It's not just sweet. Happiness applies, but it's not enough and merriment is too much. This gladness has quiet elation and thankfulness. It has humility and tenderness. It is the rare joy of true blessedness.

Did someone tell you that a baby boy
Is nothing but unadulterated joy?
Probably never knew
A boy around the age of two
Who empties wastebaskets,
Cupboards, drawers and pans,
Anything he can reach
With those busy little hands.
Who throws his food,
His spoon and cup,
And takes everything down
That should be up.
There's joy here, you bet there is.
But not all of it's yours—
some of it's his.

Watch your baby boy fall in love with you. His cries will stop when he feels your touch. He'll smile when he sees your face. He'll grasp your hair. And hug you. And he won't let go for a very long time.

The sound of a newborn's sighs are like the softest lullabies. The gurgle of a baby's giggle is like water bubbling from the freshest spring. The ring of your child's laughter is like heaven's church bells chiming just for you.

You bought him a ball
as lovely as the moon.
What does he play with?
A wooden spoon.
You bought him a teddy bear
as handsome as a king.
What does he want?
A plastic ring.
Little boys know exactly what
they want for toys.
The lids of pots,
stuffed dogs with spots,
Trucks with one wheel,
noisemakers that squeal.
In a room full of toys,
a veritable feast,
You can bet that he'll pick
the ones you like least.

Suddenly there is nothing more important than your child. Leave the room and he's still with you. The ties that bind are invisible, but strong elastic threads that bring you back before long. You are his protector, champion and playmate. And your desire is to make his new life as perfect as it can be.

Mother to a little boy,
Father to a son,
For you, as well as he,
A new life has begun.

Soon, you'll get "back to normal" after this birth of a boy. Soon, you'll feel like "yourself" again.

Very soon, you'll try to return to your "real schedule," the one before he entered the house.

But sooner or later, the truth will come to you that nothing will ever be the same. "Normal" is now and "yourself" is changing and your schedule is as "real" as the hours that disappear each day.

Life "before" and life "after" are worlds apart. Now you're a part of the world of a baby boy.

A baby boy is all innocence
  Asleep in his crib.
  But it won't be long
Before the mischief begins.
  Once he's crawling,
    Over the gates.
  Once he's walking,
    Nothing's safe.
A baby boy's idea of fun
Is to keep his parents on the run.

*It's hard to imagine
This baby boy
With snakes and turtles
And a talent to annoy.
It's hard to imagine
While he's so small
That he'll be big enough
To play basketball.
It's hard to imagine
But all too true,
That once that energy
Comes into play,
There's nothing to do
But get out of the way.*

You'll want to carry him in your arms always out of harm's way, keeping him safe. So hold him close, but let him go, too. For everywhere he turns, he'll bring new life to you.

We will try to be good parents,
but we know that love alone
is not enough.
Help us turn love into teaching,
shape love into guidance.
Lead him toward that special light
so that he may be kind,
generous, and loving;
show our son the joy of life
so he may grow toward happiness.

Colophon

Graphic Designer: Aurora C. Lyman
Typeset in Palatino, Palatino Italic and Garrick